Team Spirit

THE LOS ANGELES LAKERS

BY

MARK STEWART

Content Consultant
Matt Zeysing
Historian and Archivist
The Naismith Memorial Basketball Hall of Fame

NORWOOD HOUSE PRESS

CHICAGO, ILLINOIS

Norwood House Press
P.O. Box 316598
Chicago, Illinois 60631

For information regarding Norwood House Press, please visit our website at:
www.norwoodhousepress.com or call 866-565-2900.

All photos courtesy of AP Images—AP/Wide World Photos, Inc. except the following:
Bowman Gum Company (7 top & 14); Capital Cards (20);
Topps, Inc. (21 both, 35 right, 39 bottom, 40 top & 43);
PhotoFest (28); Bruce Hale Publications (34 right);
Author's collection (37 top); Star Company (40 bottom).
Special thanks to Topps, Inc.

Editor: Mike Kennedy
Designer: Ron Jaffe
Project Management: Black Book Partners, LLC.
Special thanks to Laura Peabody and David Ulate.

Library of Congress Cataloging-in-Publication Data

Stewart, Mark, 1960-
    The Los Angeles Lakers / by Mark Stewart ; with content consultant Matt
Zeysing.
        p. cm. -- (Team spirit)
    Summary: "Presents the history, accomplishments and key personalities of
the Los Angeles Lakers basketball team. Includes timelines, quotes, maps,
glossary and websites"--Provided by publisher.
    Includes bibliographical references and index.
    ISBN-13: 978-1-59953-068-0 (library ed. : alk. paper)
    ISBN-10: 1-59953-068-6 (library ed. : alk. paper)
    1. Los Angeles Lakers (Basketball team)--History--Juvenile literature. I.
Zeysing, Matt. II. Title. III. Series: Stewart, Mark, 1960- Team spirit.
    GV885.52.L67S74 2006
    796.323'640979494--dc22
                                                        2006015475

Manufactured in the United States of America.

COVER PHOTO: The players on the Lakers' bench rise in support
of their teammates during a 2006 Game.

Table of Contents

SPORTS WORDS & VOCABULARY WORDS: In this book, you will find many words that are new to you. You may also see familiar words used in new ways. The glossary on page 46 gives the meanings of basketball words, as well as "everyday" words that have special basketball meanings. These words appear in **bold type** throughout the book. The glossary on page 47 gives the meanings of vocabulary words that are not related to basketball. They appear in ***bold italic type*** throughout the book.

BASKETBALL SEASONS: Because each basketball season begins late in one year and ends early in the next, seasons are not named after years. Instead, they are written out as two years separated by a dash, for example 1944–45 or 2005–06.

Meet the Lakers

Most basketball fans feel lucky when their team has a great player or competes for a championship. They know that it may be years before this happens again. Fans of the Los Angeles Lakers have come to expect superstars on their team, and they demand success.

And why shouldn't they? The Lakers have had some of the best players in the history of the **National Basketball Association (NBA)**, and the team has played for the championship more than 20 times. The Lakers try to find athletes with exciting skills and big personalities, and the fans love to watch them put on a show.

This book tells the story of the Lakers. The team has built a winning *tradition* that stretches back to the 1940s. But the reason they win is that they are always looking toward the future.

Kobe Bryant gets congratulations from teammates after a game-winning shot. Bryant changed from number 8 to number 24 after the 2005–06 season.

Way Back When

Did you ever wonder why a team that plays in Los Angeles—a city on the Pacific Ocean—is called the Lakers? This is because they started in Minnesota, which is called the "Land of 10,000 Lakes." At the start of the 1947–48 season, there were three different **professional basketball** leagues competing for players

and fans. The oldest was the **National Basketball League (NBL)**, which had just placed a new team, the Lakers, in the city of Minneapolis. The Lakers were led by Jim Pollard, a well-known star in **amateur basketball**. On the sidelines was John Kundla, a popular college coach from the University of Minnesota.

Two weeks into the season, the newest of the three leagues—the **Professional Basketball League of America**—went out of business. Its best player, George Mikan, signed to play with the Lakers. Mikan wore thick glasses that made him look like Clark Kent. But he played like Superman.

With Pollard and Mikan, the Lakers were almost unbeatable. They were champions of the NBL that year, then said goodbye to the league. The Lakers and three other NBL teams joined the **Basketball Association of America (BAA)** for the 1948–49 season. Minneapolis won the championship again, and Mikan became the most famous player in basketball.

In 1949–50, the BAA joined forces with more NBL teams, and renamed itself the National Basketball Association. The name may have changed but the league champion did not—once again, the Lakers won it all. By this time, Vern Mikkelsen, a *bruising* forward, had joined Mikan and Pollard on the team's **front line**. A small guard named Slater Martin ran the offense. These four stars helped the Lakers win the NBA Championship again in 1952, 1953, and 1954.

TOP RIGHT: George Mikan   **BOTTOM RIGHT**: Mikan wonders whether he will be playing the Knicks all by himself.   **LEFT**: George Mikan gives coach John Kundla a ride after winning the 1953–54 NBA championship.

7

When these stars retired over the next few seasons, Minneapolis fans lost interest in the team. The Lakers saw the success that the Dodgers (baseball) and Rams (football) were having in Southern California, and decided to move to Los Angeles for the 1960–61 season. The Lakers had two young stars, Elgin Baylor and Jerry West, and California fans fell in love with their new team.

The Lakers reached the **NBA Finals** seven times between 1962 and 1970, but failed to win a championship. Finally, in 1972, they became NBA champions. West and Baylor were joined by center Wilt Chamberlain, guard Gail Goodrich, and coach Bill Sharman. They won an amazing 69 games during the 1971–72 season, and then beat the New York Knicks for their first championship in 18 years.

The Lakers were back on top of the basketball world in the 1980s, with a team that featured Magic Johnson, Kareem Abdul-Jabbar, James Worthy, and coach Pat Riley. Between 1980 and 1991, Los Angeles reached the NBA Finals nine times and won five championships.

LEFT: Elgin Baylor
TOP: Magic Johnson rises to the basket against the Boston Celtics.

The Team Today

With so much history and so many great players and coaches, the Lakers know the recipe for success in the NBA. A team must find an exciting shooter and **ball-handler** to run the offense, a big man to anchor the defense, and a coach who knows how to get the best out of his players. The Lakers used this plan to rebuild their team for the 21st century.

Kobe Bryant, Shaquille O'Neal, and coach Phil Jackson joined forces and won the NBA Championship in 2000, 2001, and 2002. In 2004, Jackson stepped down as coach and "Shaq" was traded for three players and two **draft choices**. When the Lakers struggled, Jackson returned to the sidelines to start shaping a new team.

If the Lakers are true to their own past, they will do whatever it takes to find a great center. However, they may decide to build a team without a seven-foot superstar—as Jackson did when he coached Michael Jordan and the Chicago Bulls during the 1990s. How the Lakers choose to work their way back to the NBA Finals will be one of the most interesting and exciting stories in basketball.

Smush Parker and Kobe Bryant jump for joy.

Home Court

When the Lakers first moved to Los Angeles, they played in a building called the Great Western Forum. The building was ringed by **Roman columns**, and was one of the fanciest sports arenas in the country.

In 1999, the team moved into the Staples Center, in downtown Los Angeles. The arena has more seats, as well as a large eight-sided scoreboard hanging over the court. It has the NBA's best sound system, which cost $1.5 million and is also used for music concerts.

The Staples Center is the only sports arena in America that is called "home" by five professional teams—the Lakers and Clippers (NBA), Sparks (WNBA), Kings (NHL), and Avengers (Arena Football). Outside of the building are larger-than-life statues of Magic Johnson and hockey star Wayne Gretzky.

STAPLES CENTER BY THE NUMBERS

- *There are 18,997 seats for basketball games in the arena.*
- *The **complex** opened on October 17, 1999.*
- *There are seven jerseys with **retired numbers** hanging in the Staples Center—13 (Wilt Chamberlain), 22 (Elgin Baylor), 25 (Gail Goodrich), 32 (Magic Johnson), 33 (Kareem Abdul-Jabbar), 42 (James Worthy), and 44 (Jerry West).*

Fans in the Staples Center celebrate the Lakers' 2000 NBA championship.

Dressed for Success

When the Lakers played in Minneapolis, their team colors reminded fans of the water and sky. The team wore bright blue and white uniforms. The team name was spelled out in **block letters** on the light-colored tops. Since the word *Minneapolis* was hard to fit across the front of a player's chest, the letters MPLS were sometimes used on the road uniforms.

The Lakers kept their blue and white colors for many years after moving to Los Angeles. Because the name of their new city could be broken into two words, it now fit nicely onto the road uniforms. In the late 1960s, the Lakers switched to the purple and gold colors

they wear today. In recent years, they have worn white home uniforms on occasion. The Lakers won nine championships after changing to purple and gold, so it is a good bet that these colors will remain part of the uniform for years to come.

Herm Schafer, a guard on the team in the 1940s, wears the Lakers' old blue and white uniform.

UNIFORM BASICS

The basketball uniform is very simple. It consists of a roomy top and baggy shorts.

- The top hangs from the shoulders, with big "scoops" for the arms and neck. This style has not changed much over the years.

- Shorts, however, have changed a lot. They used to be very short, so players could move their legs freely. In the last 20 years, shorts have actually gotten longer and much baggier.

Basketball uniforms look the same as they did long ago...until you look very closely. In the old days, the shorts had belts and buckles. The tops were made of a thick cotton called "jersey," which got very heavy when players sweated. Later, uniforms were made of shiny *satin*. They may have looked great, but they did not "breathe." Players got very hot! Today, most uniforms are made of *synthetic* materials that soak up sweat and keep the body cool.

Lamar Odom, wearing the team's home gold uniform, twists toward the hoop in a 2006 game.

We Won!

The Lakers are the only team that can claim to have won championships in three different leagues. In the days when they called Minneapolis home, they won the NBL, BAA, and NBA Finals in a span of three seasons—1947–48, 1948–49, and 1949–50. George Mikan, a big man who used his wide body and sharp elbows to move opponents out of the way, was the star of the team.

If opponents tried to put two tall defenders on Mikan, there was no one left to guard Jim Pollard. Pollard was a quick forward who was nicknamed the "Kangaroo Kid" for his incredible jumping ability. Another forward, Vern Mikkelsen, helped Mikan and Pollard with his rugged defense and rebounding.

The Lakers' first championship actually came in the winter of 1948, at the World Professional Basketball Tournament in Chicago. The top professional teams from around the country gathered to fight for the right to call themselves the best of the best. During the 1940s and early 1950s, many clubs did not belong to a league— they "barnstormed," traveling from town to town and playing for a share of the ticket sales. The best of these teams were in Chicago, too.

In the finals of the World Tournament, the Lakers defeated the New York Rens, a team made up of the best African-American players,

Jim Pollard scores a layup against the Knicks. The "Kangaroo Kid" helped the Lakers become the best team of the 1940s and early 1950s.

including Pop Gates, Duke Cumberland, George Crowe, and Nat "Sweetwater" Clifton. Mikan outscored Clifton 40 to 24, and the Lakers won 75–71.

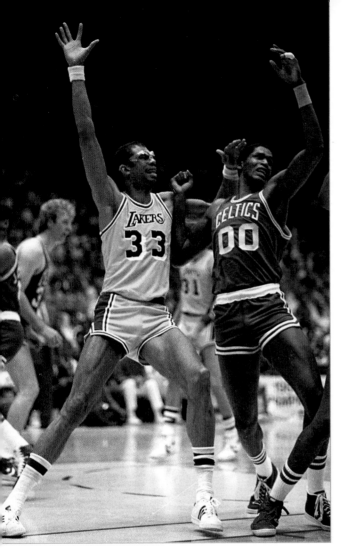

That spring, the Lakers beat Bob Davies and the Rochester Royals in the NBL Finals. The following season, after switching leagues, the Lakers beat the Washington Capitols in the BAA Finals. They won the NBA championship in 1950 against the Syracuse Nationals, then beat the New York Knicks in 1952 and 1953, and the Nationals again in 1954.

The next time the Lakers were champions, it was the 1970s, and the team had been playing in Los Angeles for many years. The 1971–72 team starred Jerry West, Wilt Chamberlain, Gail Goodrich, Jim McMillian, and Harold "Happy" Hairston. They won 69 games that season—including 33 in a row—and beat the Knicks in the NBA Finals for their first championship since moving to California. There would be many more.

Over the next 10 years, the Lakers traded for center Kareem Abdul-Jabbar and Jamaal Wilkes, and drafted Magic Johnson and

James Worthy. These four stars helped the Lakers become the best team of the 1980s. They defeated the Philadelphia 76ers in 1980 and 1982, the Boston Celtics in 1985 and 1987, and the Detroit Pistons in 1988 to add five NBA championship banners to their collection.

In 2000, Kobe Bryant and Shaquille O'Neal led the Lakers back to the NBA Finals. They defeated the Indiana Pacers to win the championship. Coach Phil Jackson surrounded these two stars with good **role players**, including Rick Fox, Derek Fisher, and Robert Horry. Los Angeles went on to win two more NBA Championships. They beat the 76ers in five games in 2001, and swept the New Jersey Nets in four games in 2002.

LEFT: Kareem Abdul-Jabbar and Robert Parish battle for position. They met in the NBA Finals three times. **ABOVE**: Shaquille O'Neal and Kobe Bryant celebrate their 2000 NBA championship.

Go-To Guys

To be a true star in the NBA, you need more than a great shot. You have to be a "go-to guy"—someone teammates trust to make the winning play when the seconds are ticking away in a big game. Lakers fans have had a lot to cheer about over the years, including these great stars...

THE PIONEERS

GEORGE MIKAN
6' 10" Center

- BORN: 6/18/1924 • DIED: 6/1/2005
- PLAYED FOR TEAM: 1947–48 TO 1953–54 & 1955–56

George Mikan used his massive body to back opponents toward the rim, where he could shoot a **hook** or layup with either hand. Mikan was so hard to defend when he got the ball close to the basket that the NBA widened the **foul lane** and created the **three-second rule** to make it harder for him to score.

JIM POLLARD
6' 4" Forward

- BORN: 7/9/1922 • DIED: 1/22/1993 • PLAYED FOR TEAM: 1947–48 TO 1954–55

Jim Pollard was an *agile* forward who could jump high for rebounds and also shoot from the outside. When opponents tried to crowd around Mikan, this often left Pollard wide open for easy shots and rebounds.

ABOVE: George Mikan
TOP RIGHT: Jerry West   **BOTTOM RIGHT**: Wilt Chamberlain

ELGIN BAYLOR   6' 5" Forward

- BORN: 9/16/1934   • PLAYED FOR TEAM: 1958–59 TO 1971–72

Elgin Baylor was the first NBA star who played "above the rim." He soared over opponents for dunks, tip-ins and rebounds. It was not unusual for him to score 30 points and grab 15 rebounds a game. Baylor's twisting, soaring shots captured the imagination of young players and fans.

JERRY WEST   6' 3" Guard

- BORN: 5/28/1938

- PLAYED FOR TEAM: 1960–61 TO 1973–74

Jerry West was one of history's best **all-around players**. He was a great defender, passer, and rebounder, and he was famous for making shots in close games. West's nickname was "Mr. **Clutch**."

WILT CHAMBERLAIN   7' 1" Center

- BORN: 8/21/1936   • DIED: 10/12/1999

- PLAYED FOR TEAM: 1968–69 TO 1972–73

Wilt Chamberlain was an incredible scorer early in his career. With the Lakers, he let his teammates do the shooting, while he focused on defense and rebounds. The Lakers went to the NBA Finals four times in the five years he wore a Los Angeles uniform.

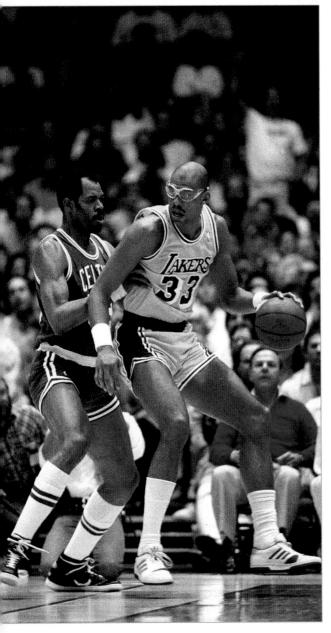

KAREEM ABDUL-JABBAR   7' 2" Center

- BORN: 4/16/1947 • PLAYED FOR TEAM: 1975–76 TO 1988–89

Kareem Abdul-Jabbar already had an NBA Championship and three **Most Valuable Player (MVP)** awards when he came to the Lakers. He earned five more championships and won three more MVPs with Los Angeles. Abdul-Jabbar retired as the NBA's all-time leading scorer with 38,387 points.

MAGIC JOHNSON   6' 9" Guard

- BORN: 8/14/1959
- PLAYED FOR TEAM: 1979–80 TO 1990–91 & 1995–96

When the Lakers drafted Magic Johnson, he was just the spark they needed to become a great team. He was like no player before him—a **point guard** in a big man's body. With his amazing skills and wonderful enthusiasm, Johnson helped Los Angeles win five championships.

ABOVE: Kareem Abdul-Jabbar
TOP RIGHT: James Worthy   **BOTTOM RIGHT**: Shaquille O'Neal

JAMES WORTHY — 6' 9" Forward

- BORN: 2/27/1961
- PLAYED FOR TEAM: 1982–83 TO 1993–94

James Worthy was one of the best all-around forwards ever to play in the NBA. When the Lakers ran their **fast break**, Worthy was often the man who finished it off with a slam dunk.

SHAQUILLE O'NEAL — 7' 1" Center

- BORN: 3/6/1972
- PLAYED FOR TEAM: 1996-97 TO 2003-04

Shaquille O'Neal was a man in search of a championship when he signed with the Lakers. He was the league's most unstoppable player, but he needed a great team to support him. "Shaq" found that and more in Los Angeles, where he won three NBA titles.

KOBE BRYANT — 6' 7" Guard

- BORN: 8/23/1978
- FIRST SEASON WITH TEAM: 1996–97

Although he was only a teenager when he joined the Lakers, Kobe Bryant was under a lot of pressure to become the NBA's next great player. He lived up to those expectations, and became one of the best to ever play the game.

On the Sidelines

The Lakers may be known for their great stars, but without a great coach, even the best players find it hard to win basketball games. Their first coach, John Kundla, knew that he could not rely entirely on his star player, George Mikan. He built a team with many different talents, which kept opponents from swarming around Mikan. The Lakers won six championships in seven seasons.

After losing in the NBA Finals seven times in a row, the Lakers hired Bill Sharman to coach the team in 1971–72. He taught the team *discipline* and made sure the players were in the best shape of their lives. They won an amazing 33 games in a row that season on the way to winning 69 games and the championship.

Pat Riley told the Lakers to play hard, have fun, and entertain the fans. They did all three, and became the best team of the 1980s. Phil Jackson asked his players to think of themselves as different parts of one great basketball creature. Some parts were more important than others, but they all had to work together to succeed. This philosophy helped the team win three championships in a row.

Coach Phil Jackson makes his point to Kobe Bryant during a timeout.

One Great Day

When Kobe Bryant has the basketball in his hands, he can score in a dozen different ways. Most NBA teams gave up trying to stop him from scoring a long time ago. They simply hope to control or *contain* him. Players around the league used to discuss what might happen if Bryant had all of his moves and all of his shots working at the same time. On a January night in Los Angeles, the Toronto Raptors found out.

Bryant was making shots from everywhere on the court—long **3-pointers**, **pull-up jump shots**, driving layups, and monster dunks. At halftime, he had 26 points. The only problem was that the Raptors were playing one of their best games of the year. When the third quarter began, Toronto held a 63–49 lead.

The Lakers kept giving the ball to Bryant, and he kept scoring. Slowly but surely, Los Angeles caught up to Toronto, and took control of the game in the fourth quarter. Everyone expected Bryant's hot shooting to cool off, but it never did. He scored 55 points in the second half to lead the Lakers to a 122–104 victory, and finished the game with 81 points!

Kobe Bryant scores two of his 81 points on a reverse layup.

Bryant's feat was truly amazing. The only time an NBA player scored more than 81 was 44 years earlier, when Wilt Chamberlain scored 100. Chamberlain was a center who towered over his opponents, and his team was far ahead in the game. Bryant, on the other hand, was challenged on every shot—and every one of his 81 points was important. "These points tonight mattered," Bryant said after the game. "We needed them."

Did Bryant think he would ever score more points in a game than Michael Jordan, Jerry West, and other great guards?

"Not even in my dreams," he smiled.

Legend Has It

LEGEND HAS IT that Kareem Abdul-Jabbar did. In the 1980 movie *Airplane*, the Lakers star played a pilot named Roger. His character caused funny misunderstandings because the word "roger" is frequently used by pilots when talking to the control tower. Abdul-Jabbar may have also been the tallest *martial arts* expert. He once fought Bruce Lee in a 1978 movie called *Game of Death*.

ABOVE: Kareem Abdul-Jabbar in *Airplane*.
RIGHT: Magic Johnson introduces Paula Abdul to the fans.

Which team cheerleader became as big a star as any of the Lakers?

LEGEND HAS IT that Paula Abdul did. For one season in the 1980s, Abdul was a Laker Girl—part of the dance team that entertains fans during halftime and timeouts. She went on to sing several Top 10 songs, and later became the only female judge on the popular television show *American Idol*.

What were the tallest baskets ever used in an NBA game?

LEGEND HAS IT that they were 12 feet high. In a 1954 game between the Lakers and Hawks, both teams agreed to play with 12-foot rims. These were two feet higher than normal. The NBA was experimenting with different ways to speed up the game. Although the Lakers won, their players agreed that the experiment was a failure. George Mikan, the tallest man on the court, missed all but two of his shots. Altogether, the Lakers made only 22 of 77 shots. Slater Martin, the shortest man on the court, had a better idea for the NBA—lower the rims to six feet. "It would make a George Mikan out of me!" he said.

It Really Happened

W hen Lakers superstar Magic Johnson stood before a room full of reporters in the fall of 1991 and announced that he was **HIV-positive**, it was one of the saddest days in sports. Fearing for his health, and the health of other players, Johnson retired from basketball to start fighting the disease.

The NBA had already printed its **All-Star ballot**, and Johnson's name was still on it. To honor him, fans all around the league voted him into the starting lineup. To their amazement, Johnson announced that he would play. Most fans thought he would just make a brief appearance. Instead, Johnson played most of the game. He scored 25 points and had nine **assists**, and led the West team to a 153–113 victory.

With less than 30 seconds left, Johnson was dribbling the ball 25 feet from the basket, guarded by his good friend, Isiah Thomas. With a big smile on his face, he whirled around and tossed up a **fade-away** 3-pointer. It looked like an impossible shot, but it went right in!

No one could play anymore after that. The players ran on the court and *embraced* Johnson. Although there were still 14 seconds left, the referees signaled that the game was over. "It was the first game ever called on account of hugs," Johnson laughed.

LEFT: Magic Johnson announces that he is HIV-positive.
ABOVE: Johnson receives the MVP award.

Team Spirit

In most NBA arenas, when a Hollywood star enters the building, it is a big event. Even the players will stop and stare. For the Lakers, playing in front of movie, music, and television *celebrities* is all part of a night's work. Their home court is only a few miles away from Hollywood, Beverly Hills, Bel Air, Santa Monica, Malibu, and other towns where the world's most famous people live and work.

The team's most loyal fan is Jack Nicholson, the award-winning actor. He sits in a courtside seat and knows as much about the Lakers as any fan in the Staples Center. He also knows most of the players personally.

Other celebrities who can be seen in the stands include Will Smith, Brad Pitt, Matthew McConaughey, Dustin Hoffman, Snoop Dogg, Alicia Keys, and Sarah Michelle Gellar. These stars love the Lakers, but there is something else they enjoy about going to games. For a few hours, they can relax, be themselves, and cheer for their favorite team just like any other fan.

Actor Jack Nicholson and singer Alicia Keys
follow the bouncing ball at a Lakers game.

Timeline

The basketball season is played from October through June. That means each season takes place at the end of one year and the beginning of the next. In this timeline, the accomplishments of the Lakers are shown by season.

1947–48
The Lakers join the National Basketball League.

1968–69
Jerry West is named NBA Finals MVP in a loss to the Boston Celtics.

1953–54
The Lakers win the NBA Finals for the third time in a row.

1960–61
The Lakers move to Los Angeles.

1971–72
The Lakers win their first championship in Los Angeles.

George Mikan

Wilt Chamberlain scores against the New York Knicks in the 1972 NBA Finals.

Kareem Abdul-Jabbar

Kobe Bryant and Shaquille O'Neal

1975–76
The Lakers trade for Kareem Abdul-Jabbar.

1999–00
Shaquille O'Neal and Kobe Bryant lead the Lakers to the championship.

1979–80
The Lakers draft Magic Johnson.

1987–88
The Lakers win their fifth championship of the 1980s.

2002–03
Kobe Bryant leads the NBA with 2,461 points.

Kobe Bryant floats to the rim for a two-handed dunk.

Fun Facts

LITTLE BIG MAN

In Game Six of the 1980 NBA Finals, **rookie** guard Magic Johnson took the place of injured center Kareem Abdul-Jabbar. He scored

42 points and grabbed 15 rebounds to lead the Lakers to the championship.

UNSTOPPABLE!

The Lakers' 33-game winning streak during the 1971–72 season is still the longest ever for a team in a major sport.

MR. LOGO

The red-white-and-blue NBA *logo* has the outline of a player dribbling a basketball. Many believe that Jerry West of the Lakers was the "model" for this player.

IT'S CLEAR NOW

Slater Martin was one of only two NBA players to wear glass contact lenses during the 1950s.

THAT'S THE TICKET

In between their NBA games, the Lakers sometimes played in **exhibition doubleheaders**. The players made extra money and helped pro basketball become more popular.

SWEET DEAL

The best trade in team history occurred in 1996. The Lakers traded center Vlade Divac to the Charlotte Hornets for 18-year-old Kobe Bryant. This move also gave the team enough money to sign Shaquille O'Neal!

LOVE THAT LAKER

For many years, one of the biggest celebrities in the seats at Lakers games was actress and singer Vanessa Williams. Her husband, Rick Fox, was a member of three championship teams.

TOP: A ticket from a 1950 Lakers exhibition.
The Harlem Globetrotters also appeared in this doubleheader.
ABOVE: Vanessa Williams and Rick Fox   **LEFT**: Jerry West

Talking Hoops

"We play as a team.
One-man teams are losing teams."
—*Kareem Abdul-Jabbar, on how
the Lakers became champions*

"Weaknesses stand out like
a ***neon sign***. So just don't
practice your strengths.
Practice your weaknesses."
—*Magic Johnson, on the
key to improving*

"Winning a championship
is never easy. And it *shouldn't* be."
—*Phil Jackson, on the rewards
of hard work*

ABOVE: Phil Jackson
TOP RIGHT: Kobe Bryant   **BOTTOM RIGHT**: Jerry West

"I'll do whatever it takes to win games, whether it's sitting on a bench waving a towel, handing a cup of water to a teammate, or hitting the game-winning shot."

—*Kobe Bryant, on how a star contributes*

"Any team can be a miracle team— but you have to go out and work for your miracles."

—*Pat Riley, on the secret behind winning teams*

"Good balance is necessary to shoot the jumper or any other shot. No shot is a good percentage shot—no matter how close to the hoop—if it's taken from an awkward position."

—*Jerry West, on having the correct shooting form*

39

For the Record

The great Lakers teams and players have left their marks on the record books. These are the "best of the best"…

Elgin Baylor

Magic Johnson

LAKERS AWARD WINNERS

WINNER	AWARD	SEASON
George Mikan	All-Star Game MVP	1952–53
Elgin Baylor	All-Star Game Co-MVP	1958–59
Elgin Baylor	Rookie of the Year*	1958–59
Jerry West	NBA Finals MVP	1968–69
Jerry West	All-Star Game MVP	1971–72
Wilt Chamberlain	NBA Finals MVP	1971–72
Bill Sharman	Coach of the Year	1971–72
Kareem Abdul-Jabbar	NBA MVP	1975–76
Kareem Abdul-Jabbar	NBA MVP	1976–77
Magic Johnson	NBA Finals MVP	1979–80
Kareem Abdul-Jabbar	NBA MVP	1979–80
Magic Johnson	NBA Finals MVP	1981–82
Kareem Abdul-Jabbar	NBA Finals MVP	1984–85
Michael Cooper	Defensive Player of the Year	1986–87
Magic Johnson	NBA Finals MVP	1986–87
Magic Johnson	NBA MVP	1986–87
James Worthy	NBA Finals MVP	1987–88
Magic Johnson	NBA MVP	1988–89
Magic Johnson	All-Star Game MVP	1989–90
Magic Johnson	NBA MVP	1989–90
Pat Riley	Coach of the Year	1989–90
Magic Johnson	All-Star Game MVP	1991–92
Del Harris	Coach of the Year	1994–95
Shaquille O'Neal	All-Star Game Co-MVP	1999–00
Shaquille O'Neal	NBA Finals MVP	1999–00
Shaquille O'Neal	NBA MVP	1999–00
Shaquille O'Neal	NBA Finals MVP	2000–01
Kobe Bryant	All-Star Game MVP	2001–02
Shaquille O'Neal	NBA Finals MVP	2001–02
Shaquille O'Neal	All-Star Game MVP	2003–04

The Rookie of the Year award is given to the league's best first-year player.

LAKERS ACHIEVEMENTS

ACHIEVEMENT	SEASON
NBL Champions	1947–48
BAA Champions	1948–49
NBA Champions	1949–50
NBA Champions	1951–52
NBA Champions	1952–53
NBA Champions	1953–54
NBA Champions	1971–72
NBA Champions	1979–80
NBA Champions	1981–82
NBA Champions	1984–85
NBA Champions	1986–87
NBA Champions	1987–88
NBA Champions	1999–00
NBA Champions	2000–01
NBA Champions	2001–02

TOP: George Mikan shows off his many trophies.
ABOVE: Magic Johnson and Pat Riley pose with Johnson's 1982 Finals MVP trophy.
LEFT: Phil Jackson and Shaquille O'Neal plan their next move.

Pinpoints

The history of a basketball team is made up of many smaller stories. These stories take place all over the map—not just in the city a team calls "home." Match the push-pins on these maps to the Team Facts and you will begin to see the story of the Lakers unfold!

TEAM FACTS

1   Los Angeles, California—*The Lakers have played here since 1960.*

2   Berkeley, California—*Jamaal Wilkes was born here.*

3   Deer Lodge, Montana—*Phil Jackson was born here.*

4   Minneapolis, Minnesota—*The Lakers played here from 1947 to 1960.*

5   Joliet, Illinois—*George Mikan was born here.*

6   Rome, New York—*Pat Riley was born here.*

7   New York, New York—*Kareem Abdul-Jabbar was born here.*

8   Philadelphia, Pennsylvania—*Kobe Bryant was born here.*

9   Washington, D.C.—*Elgin Baylor was born here.*

10   Cheylan, West Virginia—*Jerry West was born here.*

11   Gastonia, North Carolina—*James Worthy was born here.*

12   Prijepolje, Yugoslavia—*Vlade Divac was born here.*

Vlade Divac

Play Ball

Basketball is a sport played by two teams of five players. NBA games have four 12-minute quarters—48 minutes in all—and the team that scores the most points when time has run out is the winner. Most baskets count for two points. Players who make shots from beyond the three-point line receive an extra point. Baskets made from the free-throw line count for one point. Free throws are penalty shots awarded to a team, usually after an opponent has committed a foul. A foul is called when one player makes hard contact with another.

Players can move around all they want, but the player with the ball cannot. He must bounce the ball with one hand or the other (but never both) in order to go from one part of the court to another. As long as he keeps "dribbling," he can keep moving.

In the NBA, teams must attempt a shot every 24 seconds, so there is little time to waste. The job of the defense is to make it as difficult as possible to take a good shot—and to grab the ball if the other team shoots and misses.

This may sound simple, but anyone who has played the game knows that basketball can be very complicated. Every player on the court has a job to do. Different players have different strengths and weaknesses. The coach must mix these players in just the right way, and teach them to work together as one.

The more you play and watch basketball, the more "little things" you are likely to notice. The next time you are at a game, look for these plays:

ALLEY-OOP—A play where the passer throws the ball just to the side of the rim—so a teammate can catch it and dunk in one motion.

BACK-DOOR PLAY—A play where the passer waits for his teammate to fake the defender away from the basket—then throws him the ball when he cuts back toward the basket.

KICK-OUT—A play where the ball-handler waits for the defense to surround him—then quickly passes to a teammate who is open for an outside shot. The ball is not really kicked in this play; the term comes from the action of pinball machines.

NO-LOOK PASS—A play where the passer fools a defender (with his eyes) into covering one teammate—then suddenly passes to another without looking.

PICK-AND-ROLL—A play where one teammate blocks or "picks off" another's defender with his body—then cuts to the basket for a pass in the confusion.

Glossary

3-POINTERS—Shots made from behind the 3-point line.

ALL-AROUND PLAYERS—Players good at all parts of basketball.

ALL-STAR BALLOT—A piece of paper fans use to vote for the players they would like to see in the NBA's annual All-Star Game.

AMATEUR BASKETBALL—Basketball played by people who are not paid. This includes high-school and college players. From the 1920s to the 1950s, many top amateurs played for company teams.

ASSISTS—Passes that lead to successful shots.

BALL-HANDLER—Someone good at dribbling and passing.

BASKETBALL ASSOCIATION OF AMERICA (BAA)—The league that joined forces with the NBL and became the National Basketball Association. The league's championship series was the BAA Finals.

CLUTCH—Able to perform under pressure, or "in the clutch."

DRAFT CHOICES—Players picked during the meeting each year at which NBA teams take turns choosing the best amateur and foreign players.

EXHIBITION DOUBLEHEADERS—A set of two games, played one after the other, that do not count in the standings. Exhibition games are now played before the regular season starts.

FADE-AWAY—A shot taken while jumping away from the basket.

FAST BREAK—A play where the offensive team breaks quickly down the court.

FOUL LANE—The painted rectangular area in front of the basket. Players must stand on either side while someone is taking a free throw.

FRONT LINE—A team's two forwards and center.

HOOK—A one-handed shot taken with the shooter's body between the defender and the ball.

MOST VALUABLE PLAYER (MVP)—An award given each year to the league's best player; also given to the top player in the league finals and All-Star Game.

NATIONAL BASKETBALL ASSOCIATION (NBA)—The professional league that has been operating since 1946–47.

NATIONAL BASKETBALL LEAGUE (NBL)—The professional league that started in 1937-38 and later joined forces with the NBA. The league's championship series was the NBL Finals.

NBA FINALS—The playoff series that decides the championship of the league.

POINT GUARD—The player whose job it is to guide the team on the court and start plays on offense.

PROFESSIONAL BASKETBALL—Basketball played for money. College and high school players are not paid, so they are considered "amateurs." Professional players are sometimes called "pros."

PROFESSIONAL BASKETBALL LEAGUE OF AMERICA—A pro league that failed soon after it began in 1947.

PULL-UP JUMP SHOTS—Shots taken after stopping suddenly and rising into the air.

RETIRED NUMBERS—Uniform numbers that a team has decided no one else will ever wear.

ROLE PLAYERS—People who are asked to do specific things when they are in a game.

ROOKIE—A player in his first season.

THREE-SECOND RULE—A rule that limits the time a player can stand in the foul lane to three seconds.

OTHER WORDS TO KNOW

AGILE—Quick and graceful.

BLOCK LETTERS—Big, squared-off letters.

BRUISING—Rough enough to cause bruises.

CELEBRITIES—People who are very famous.

COMPLEX—A group of buildings.

CONTAIN—To hold back or limit.

DISCIPLINE—The training of the mind and body according to a set of rules.

EMBRACED—Held closely in one's arms.

HIV-POSITIVE—Infected with the AIDS virus.

LOGO—A symbol or design that represents a business or team.

MARTIAL ARTS—A group of special fighting styles.

NEON SIGN—A bright, glowing, electric sign.

ROMAN COLUMNS—An ancient building design sometimes used in modern architecture.

SATIN—A smooth, shiny fabric.

SYNTHETIC—Made in a laboratory, not in nature.

TRADITION—A belief or custom passed down from generation to generation.

Places to Go

ON THE ROAD

STAPLES CENTER
1111 South Figueroa Street
Los Angeles, California   90015
(213) 742-7300

NAISMITH MEMORIAL BASKETBALL HALL OF FAME
1000 West Columbus Avenue
Springfield, Massachusetts 01105
(877) 4HOOPLA

ON THE WEB

THE NATIONAL BASKETBALL ASSOCIATION   www.nba.com
  • *to learn more about the league's teams, players, and history*

THE LOS ANGELES LAKERS   www.Lakers.com
  • *to learn more about the Los Angeles Lakers*

THE BASKETBALL HALL OF FAME   www.hoophall.com
  • *to learn more about history's greatest players*

ON THE BOOKSHELF

To learn more about the sport of basketball, look for these books at your library or bookstore:

  • Hareas, John. *Basketball*. New York, NY: DK, 2005.

  • Hughes, Morgan. *Basketball*. Vero Beach, FL: Rourke Publishing, 2005.

  • Thomas, Keltie. *How Basketball Works*. Berkeley, CA: Maple Tree Press, distributed through Publishers Group West, 2005.

47

Index

The Team

, MARK STEWART has written more than 20 books on basketball, and over 100 sports books for kids. He grew up in New York City during the 1960s rooting for the Knicks and Nets, and now takes his two daughters, Mariah and Rachel, to watch them play. Mark comes from a family of writers. His grandfather was Sunday Editor of *The New York Times* and his mother was Articles Editor of *The Ladies Home Journal* and *McCall's*. Mark has profiled hundreds of athletes over the last 20 years. He has also written several books about his native New York, and New Jersey, his home today. Mark is a graduate of Duke University, with a degree in history. He lives with his daughters and wife, Sarah, overlooking Sandy Hook, NJ.

MATT ZEYSING is the resident historian at the Basketball Hall of Fame in Springfield, Massachusetts. His research interests include the origins of the game of basketball, the development of professional basketball in the first half of the twentieth century, and the culture and meaning of basketball in American society.